WHAT'S A DADDY FOR ?

Written By Pat Snyder
Photos by Paige Telep
Book Layout by Steven Himes

Nana's Publishing ©2015

I0157643

WHAT'S A DADDY FOR?

Written By Pat Snyder
Photos by Paige Telep
Book Layout by Steven Himes

Nana's Publishing
© Copyright May, 2015

International Standard Book Number
ISBN-13: 978-0692451205
ISBN-10: 069245120X

Library of Congress Number
2015908123

All rights reserved. No portion of this book may be reproduced, stored in a retrieval system, or transmitted in any form or by any means – electronic, mechanical, photocopy, recording, scanning, or other ---except for brief quotations in critical reviews or articles, without the prior written permission of the author.

When Michael was a tiny tot
Before he could speak a word
He had **deep** thoughts and *wonderings*
About things in this world.

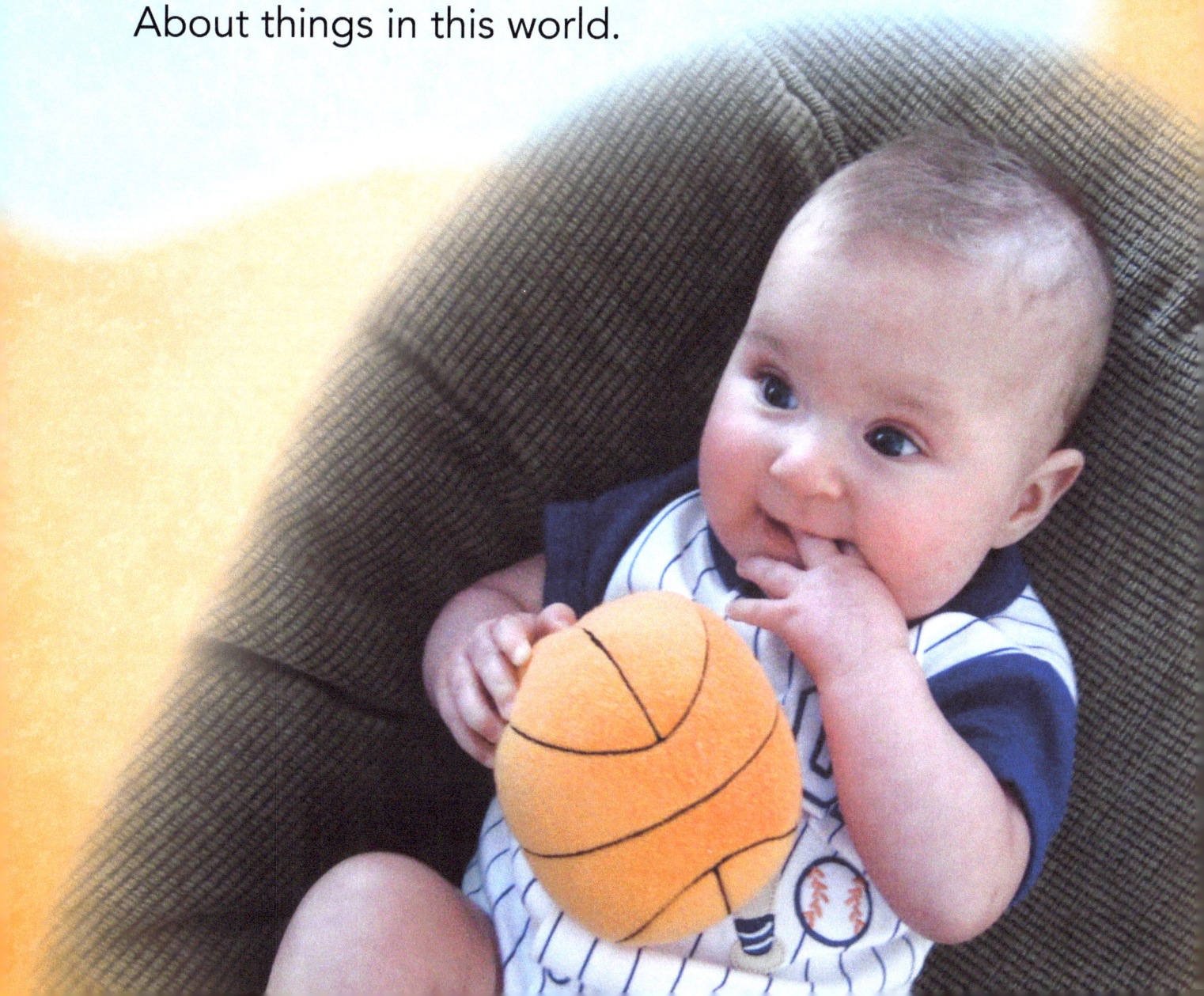

He'd figured out who **Mommy** was
And how she made him *feel*.

He'd learned to get the things he needed
With a **cry**, a *laugh*, or a ***squeal***.

He understood about his room,
His bed, his bath, his clothes.
But there was still one **giant** thing
That Michael wanted to know.

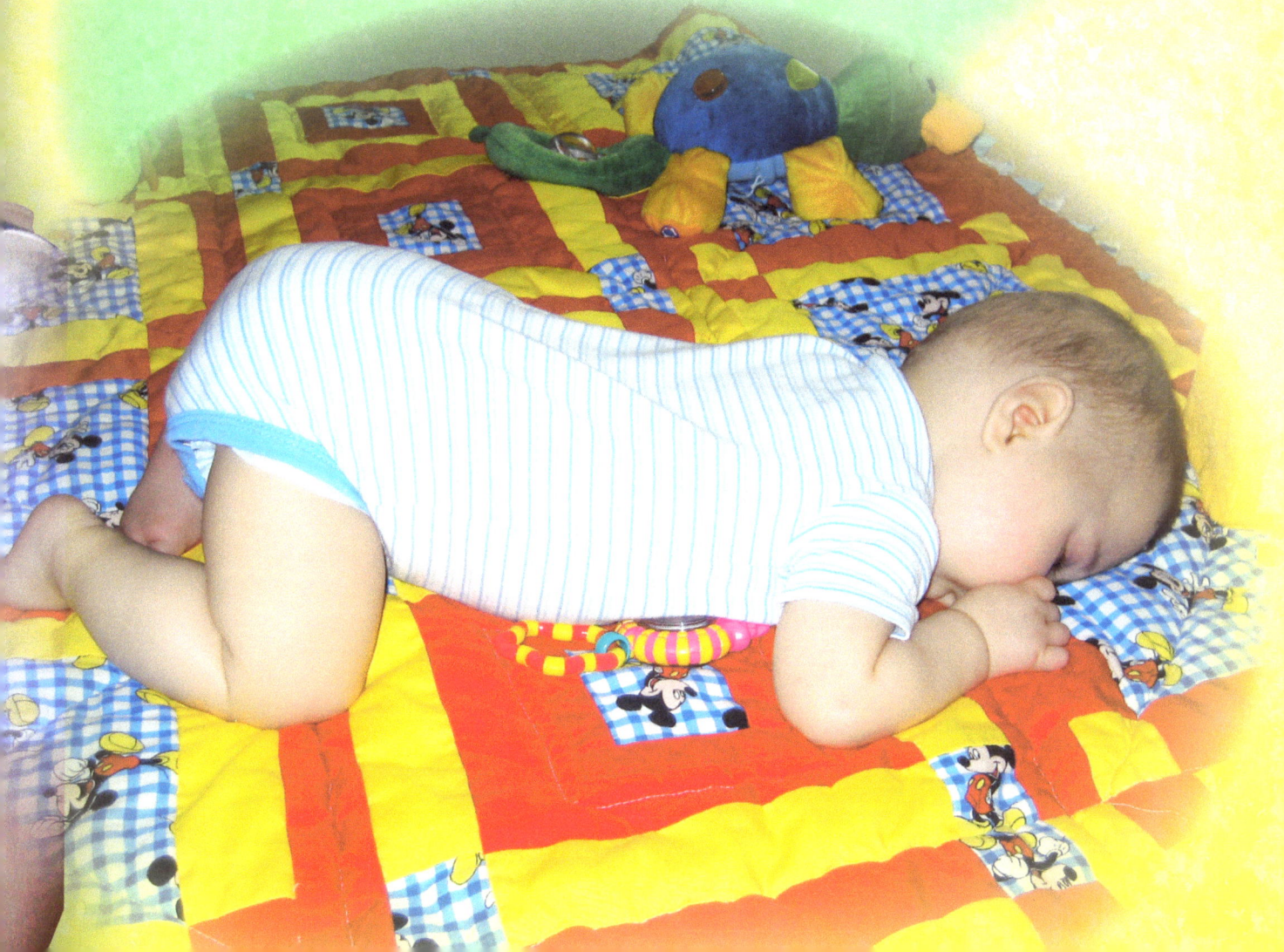

There was a man who looked like him,
But **taller** and **bigger** and **more**.

When Michael saw him, he always thought,
"What's a Daddy for?"

He **watched** and he *listened*
As his dad lifted him to the ceiling.

Dad hung him upside down and *laughed*,
Giving Michael a ***dizzy*** feeling.

His Mommy's face was always *s m o o t h*;
His Daddy's was sometimes **rough**.
His Mommy's voice was *gentle* and *soft*;
His Daddy's could be **deep**, **loud**, and **gruff**.

Why would he need a **scratchy** beard?
Why would he need a **deep voice**?

Why would **rough** play be important to him?
Did he have to make some choice?

"**What is a Daddy for?**" he thought,
"**Why do I need one of those?**"

Can't I get by with just a **Mom**?
What is it **Daddy** knows?"

His dad **jumped** up and tossed him **high**.
This ***thrilled*** Michael from head to toe.

He **bounced** little Mike on both his knees
And said, **"Son, there are some things I know."**

"I know that you need a *gentle*, **strong** man
To teach you what's right from the start.

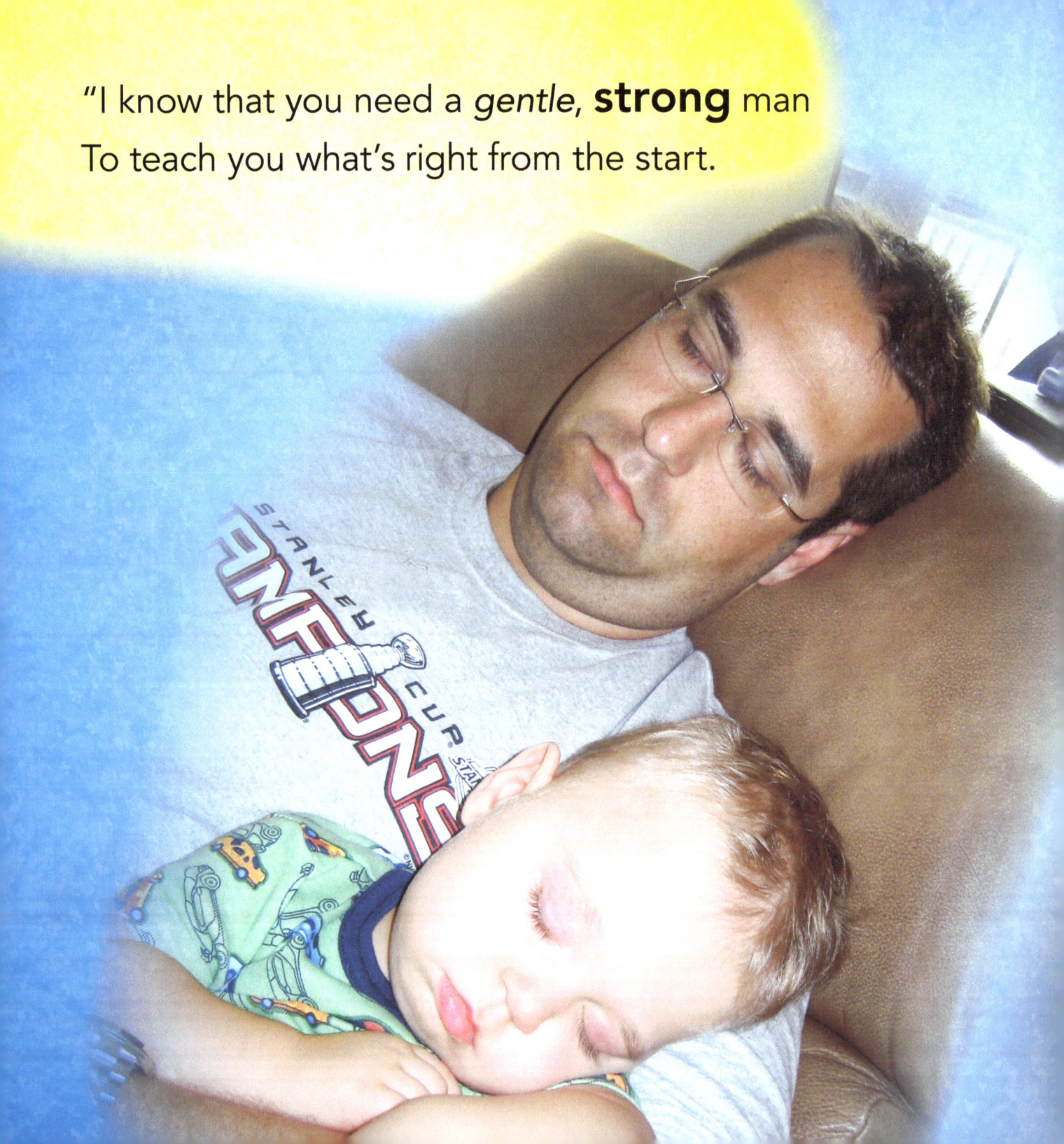

To guide by example, to keep a *cool head*,
To always **lead with your heart**."

"It's **vital** to know how to **win** and to **lose**---
As a **gentleman** how to compete.

A **dad** helps you see that the game is *like life*.
A **dad** makes the **son** more *complete*."

"A boy needs a *balance*---a **mom** and a **dad**
To build a strong **foundation** and *more*."

Michael just smiled as he thought to himself,
"Now I know what my Daddy is for!"

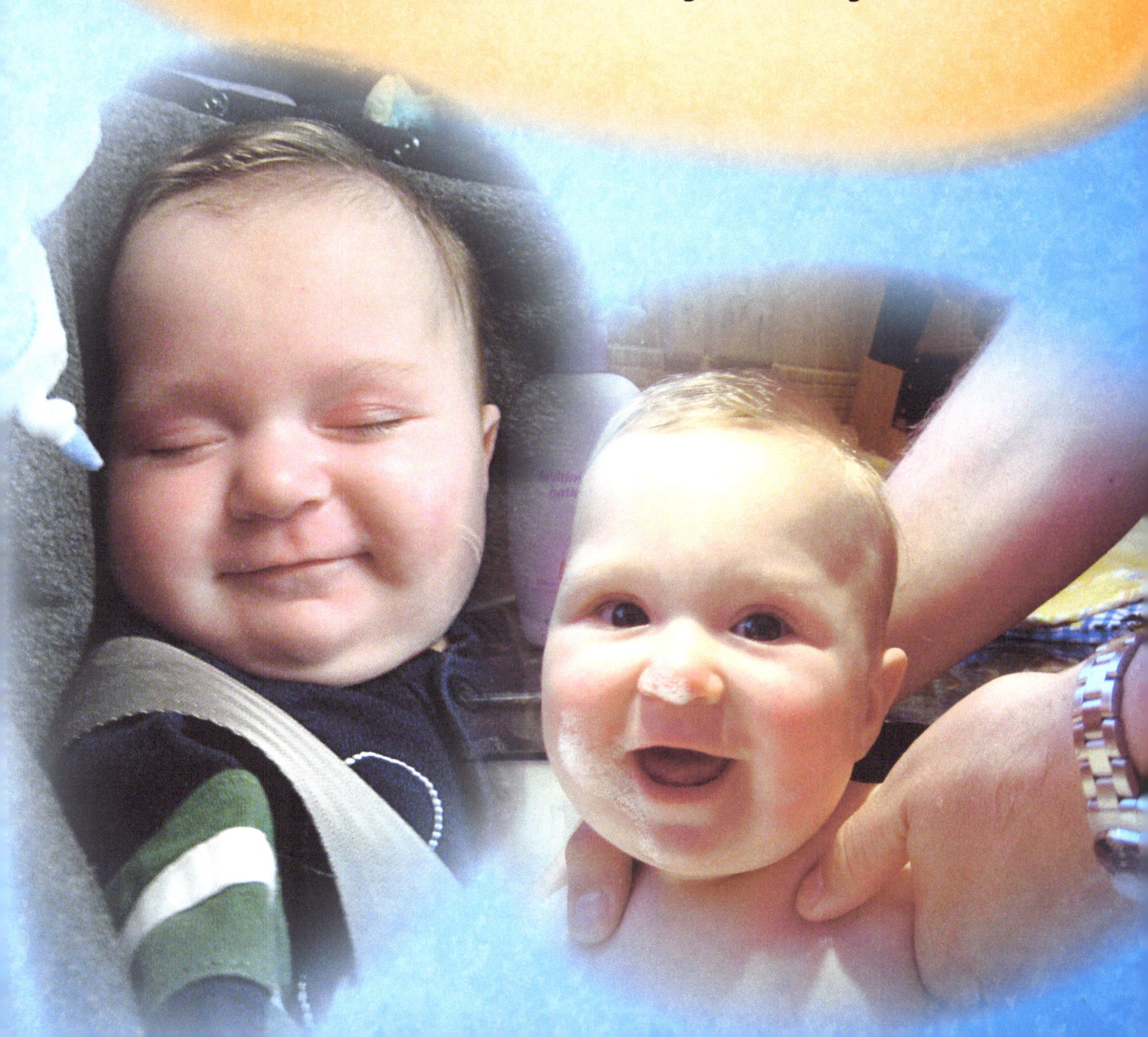

It all starts with great teaching...

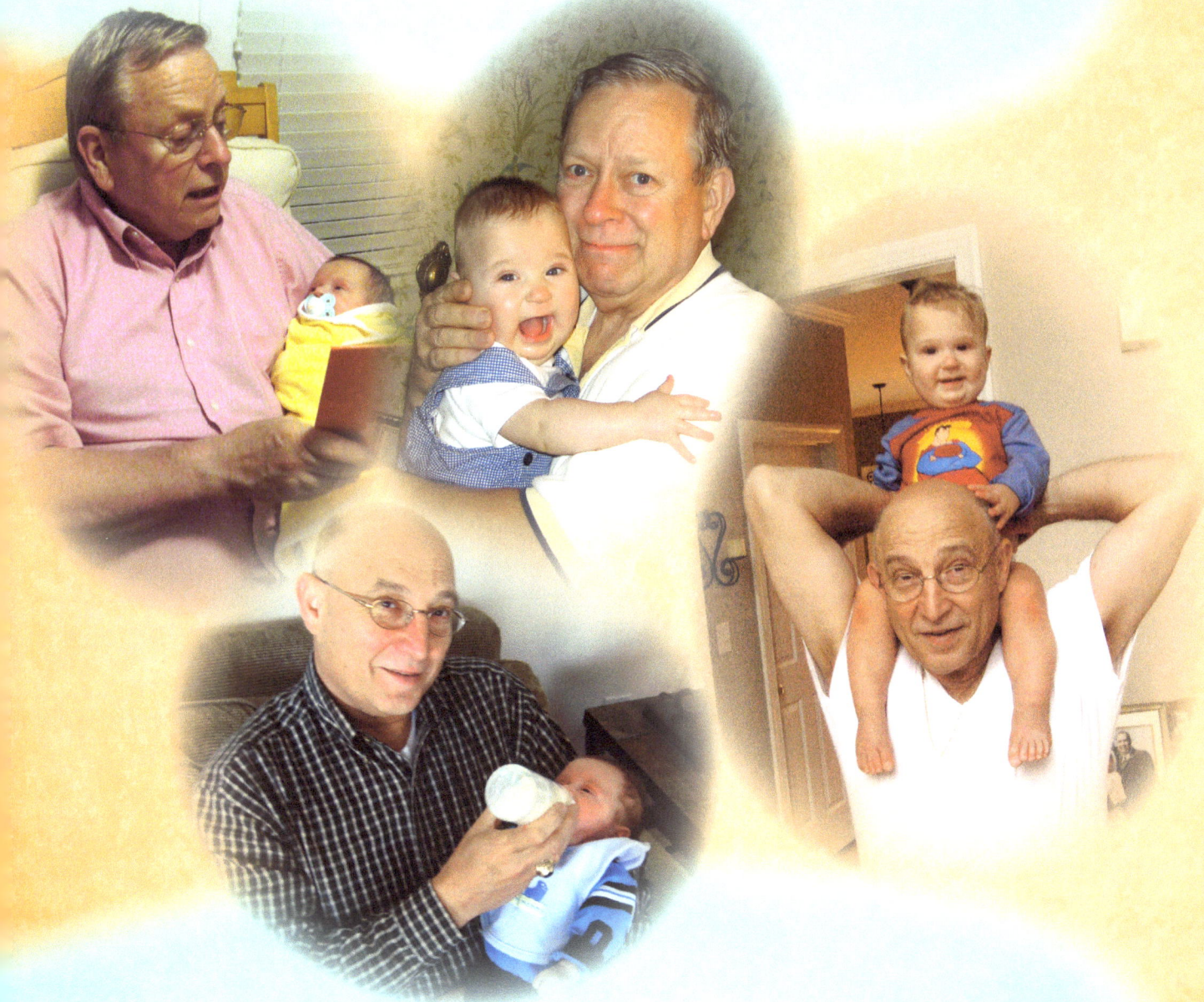

...from Grandfathers!

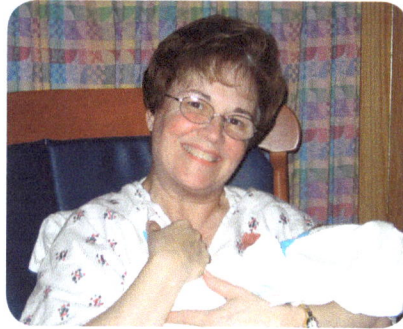

ABOUT THE AUTHOR

Pat Snyder, who lives in North Carolina,
is author of *"Treasures in the Darkness"*.
This is her first children's book.

To contact Pat Snyder, please email her at
patsnyder137@gmail.com.

Find *"Treasures in the Darkness"* and more copies
of *"What's a Daddy For?"* on Amazon.com.

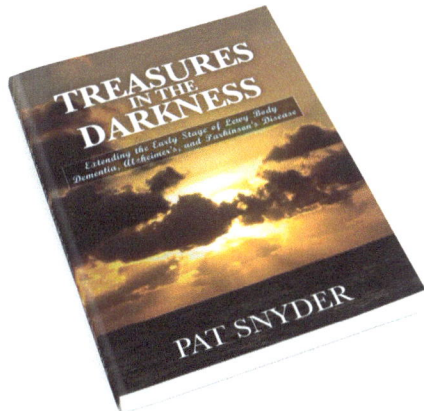
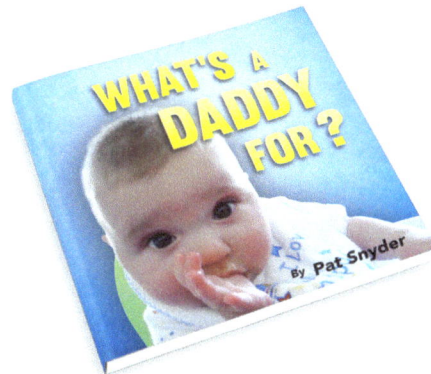

www.ingramcontent.com/pod-product-compliance
Lightning Source LLC
Chambersburg PA
CBHW042113040426
42448CB00002B/262